GLADINE P. BRUER

PROISLE PUBLISHING

© COPYRIGHT 2024 BY GLADINE P. BRUER

ISBN: 978-1-963735-50-5

All rights reserved. No part of this book may be reproduced or transmitted in any form or by any means, electronic or mechanical, including photocopying, recording, or by any information storage and retrieval system, without permission in writing from the copyright owner.

The views expressed in this work are solely those of the author and do not necessarily reflect the views of the publisher, and the publisher disclaims any responsibility for them.

To order additional copies of this book, contact:

Proisle Publishing Services LLC
39-67 58th Street, 1st floor
Woodside, NY 11377, USA
Phone: (+1 646-480-0129)
info@proislepublishing.com

~INTRODUCTION~

Through the eyes of my JOY is a book filled with thoughts and admiration of my Family, Friends, and Acquaintances, who have walked down the path of my life in so many positive directions, following the LORD.

The cover is a beautiful picture of a child (my #1 grand daughter—Naomi Karin Robinson) with the purest look: the look from a Child, the sincerest look of all times.

P.S. The definition of Naomi —IS JOY— and all seven of my grands they are My Joy
(Carl[#3] – D'Andre – Avery – Tyler – Naomi – Caiden & Carmela)

TABLE OF CONTENTS

Poetry — 9
Inner Peace — 10
Baby Boy! — 11
The Smile of an Empty Face — 12
A Cold Man in Your Day — 13
By Chance — 14
Where Shall I Be? — 15
Watching You — 16
The Peaceful Man — 17
Seasons — 18
What's in One's Heart — 19
God First — 20
Pages of Your Life (Taken from the Wordless Book) — 21
D — 23
Mama Anna — 24
WELL DONE! — 25
Little Fellas — 27
Ms. Hicks — 29
Are You Unhappy? — 30
AMBIVALENCE — 31
The RAIN — 32
Antithesis — 33
Special that's YOU — 34
Setting One's Mind — 35
Who is D — 36
Such Memories — 37
Powers is Patience — 38
Impressions or Directions — 39
Media Madness — 40
Just A Smile — 41
Exhale or Inhale — 42

POETRY

What is Poetry to me?

A feeling of inspiration
A cup of soul temptation

Poetry, a glance at the stars
Motions of the ocean from afar.

An urge to express
A smile from the lips,
A gleam from the eye.
Poetry helps with the where,
when and why?

Capture the feeling you really felt.
with poetry,
One's heart just melt!

Soothing gestures,
Kind thoughts of Thee,
This is What Poetry is to me!

Gladine Bruer

Through the Eyes of My Joy

INNER PEACE

Cool ripples of water in a stream
Gives me Inner Peace

An inspirational Book to read
Gives me Inner Peace

Thoughts of God's Word
Gives me Inner Peace

Focusing on Peace within
Thoughts that are Good
Not of sin

Inner Peace restores the soul

Inner Peace
My Ultimate Goal!!!

Gladine Pannell Bruer – March 20, 2007

Through the Eyes of My Joy

BABY BOY!

This poem is to my Baby Boy
Who looks at life as one big Toy
That's Okay – I understand
But you're all grown up, so be a Man
Take care of what is precious to you
Tyler, Avery, and number 3—Pooh
Let's not forget old Mom and Dad,
Dee and Mike, that would be so sad!
Take care and remember your legacy
And how you will want it to be
Bad or Good, Dark or Bright, False or True
Baby Boy it's all up to you
Respect and Honor – Are you due these things?
Because this, Baby Boy, is what a legacy Brings

Love,
Mom

Forever to My Baby Boy
(Carl L. Bruer, Jr.)

Gladine Pannell Bruer – 2012

Through the Eyes of My Joy

THE SMILE OF AN EMPTY FACE

Look in the Mirror
The stare is long overdue!

What do you see?
A face – An empty Face!

Is there a frown or a smile on this face?
Which would you like to see?

Frowns full of neglect and sorrow
Or
Smiles that will fill up the empty face?

Smiles fill the emptiness of a face.

To ALL the empty faces in this world
God be your guide.

By Gladine Pannel Bruer – January 2007

Through the Eyes of My Joy

A COLD MAN IN YOUR DAY

As time passes me by
I can feel the chill
Days gone by – No big deal

As brisk and as cold as a winter breeze
A cold man in your day
I do believe

To deny, and say things that really hurt
Memory brings them back in little spurts

The flouncing of the hussies pale
It's a wonder I didn't go to jail

A cold man in your day
No smile, no laughs, no time to play

A cold man you were
IN YOUR DAY!!!

Gladine Pannell Bruer – October 2006

Through the Eyes of My Joy

BY CHANCE

By chance did you wake up today?
By chance did you give thanks and pray?

By chance are you in good health?
By chance is your life full of wealth?

By chance are you in control?
By chance can you see the writing Bold?
By chance have you rendered your soul?
By chance are you young or old?

By chance can you ask for forgiveness?

If by chance the answer is yes
By chance, you've passed the Lord's test
And Only
By chance!!!

Gladine Pannell Bruer – October 2006

WHERE SHALL I BE?

As I gaze out into the Trees
I ask myself *Where Shall I be?*

I wonder down the path of life
Thinking about the world's hard strife

The daughter role I've played that part
Remembering my mother's heart

Sister, I'll always cherish
For her love, it just flourish

Wife, I guess I am okay
I kept my mind from day to day

Mother, now that's a spot
Being strong it takes a lot

Life, it opens doors you see
That's why I ask
Where Shall I Be????

Gladine Pannell Bruer – May 2006

Through the Eyes of My Joy
WATCHING YOU

Watching you grow up so fine
Makes me smile just all the time
I think of all the fun we've had
And boy it makes me oh so glad

To know that we still have some time
And here I am near my prime
Life can be oh-so-nice
When you can get one big slice

A smile, a laugh, a cry or two
I cherish these I've had with you
And now you will get your turn
To Live, To Love, and also Learn
That children are a GOD send
This I offer friend-to-friend

As I close with pleasant thoughts
You're on my mind and in my mind

A blessed addition to our world
Whether it be Boy or Girl(???)
Will just give my Life another Whirl

Love Forever
Mommy!!!!!!

This Poem is dedicated to my daughter:
Denitra Lynn Bruer-Robinson
06/27/2006
GPB (Gladine Parnell Bruer)
Thanks for being You.

THE PEACEFUL MAN

The kind of man you would want for a Son
Who would always be there when the morning comes

The kind of man you would want for a brother
Who cherished his sibling, grandmother and mother

The kind of man you would want for a Soulmate
Aunt Gloria knows—he was her permanent date

The kind of man you would want for a Dad!
Just asked his children,
he was there when they were happy or sad

All these thngs about The Peaceful Man
and what does this man mean to me?

He is my uncle Lonnie
The Peaceful Man

Always,
Gla

SEASONS

Seasons are like spices
They have their time.
And with the right ingredients
You can have something divine

The Winter brings the snow so bright
With Spring comes the cool of night
Summer is the heat and sun
With it comes so much fun
But best, I think, is the Fall
Perfect time for one and All

Seasons, the variety of Life

Gladine Pannell Bruer – 2008

Through the Eyes of My Joy

WHAT'S IN ONE'S HEART

What's in one's heart in this God's world.|?
Intimacy for others should be clear as a Pearl!
Know that the Lord really does care
What's in your heart, please stop and Share.

Don't be Distracted, Doubtful or Discouraged
Stop all that Whimpering, Crying and Worrying.
Don't waste Precious Time
While you're in your Prime.

Extravagant Love within one's heart
Gratitude, not Greed, is the Total Part
Faith you must have from day to day
On a steady path, one must Stay

The Lord is where we shall Start.
So we all will know
What's in one's Heart!

Dedicated to: The Women's Sunday School Class and Fellowship at Grace Bible Church Charles, WV

Gladine Pannell Bruer – May 22, 2012

GOD FIRST

As life passes with such great haste
Time for salvation we do waste
In need of food or water your thirst
Always remember

GOD FIRST

You wake up to the morning Glory
Before the day ends – you have a story
Light of day and dark of night

GOD FIRST

Or Life just ain't right
Do your best – not your worst
Remember to keep
GOD FIRST!!!

Gladine Pannell Bruer – March 20, 2007

PAGES OF YOUR LIFE
(TAKEN FROM THE WORDLESS BOOK)

The Golden Page is heaven-sent
The Holy Creator God is there in print
As we all know, he loves us all
Small, medium, large or tall
As we all confess that we have sinned
The Lord helps us begin again
Because we all know in heaven – No Sin!!!
So on to the Dark Page where we've all been
Sin, as we know, is Born within
Red is the page where this begins
Jesus, God's Perfect Son
Died, buried and rose again
Took the punishment for our sin

Thinking, saying and doing bad things
To God's strong heart, sadness it brings
God has a plan for you and me
He will be there to help thee
The Clean Page is all yours.
Admit you're a sinner–make him smile
Believe in the Lord with every mile
Choose God in your Life and you will Grow
Green as the grass we all know

Through the Eyes of My Joy

Go to church regularly
Read your Bible wholeheartedly
Obey and respect, that's his call
Witness his word to one and all
Last but not least, Day after Day
Stop and take the time to Pray
In regards to the Wordless Book

As God's child, you should be hooked
If you're going through pain and strife
Try making these Pages
A part of your LIFE

Gladine Pannell Bruer – March 19, 2007

Through the Eyes of My Joy

D

D-My one and only girl
A breath of sunshine in my world.
D-termined to pass every test
D-my daughter, she's the best
D-sire to respect and love all
D-Four ft. 11" but stand so tall
D-serving of so many things
D-cide to take what life will bring
D-lightful as a song you sing
D-she is my everything

To Denitra

Gla – May 2006

Through the Eyes of My Joy

MAMA ANNA
DEDICATED TO A LADY WHO IMPACTED MY LIFE IN SO MANY WAYS

A lady of love

A lady of kindness

A lady with class

Who's been a part of my past

Always with a smile on her face

I could always enjoy her in any place

At Church, at Fellowship and even the Mall

Oh, Mama Anna, we had a ball!!!

I will always remember the wisdom she shared

I will always know that she really cared

So lay your head down and get your rest

Because we all know God picks only the best

So Mama Anna, I won't say goodbye

And I will try real hard not to cry

I'll just throw you a kiss with a smile and a sigh

As my Mama Anna goes to heaven on high!!

"Anna Stovall Dorcas --- May 6, 2000"

Gladine Pannell. Bruer

Through the Eyes of My Joy

WELL DONE!

As we enter into this world
Little boy or little girl
Not knowing any of the fads
Not even knowing Mom or Dad

Look around, all is strange
Boy is your life about to change
No more closeness to Mama's breast
You think you will pass the Test?

Trials, Truths and manmade gadgets
Movie Stars and Beauty Pageants
Money, riches and material things
Fur coats, clothes and diamond rings

Oh the temptations this life brings
Lord, you will be wanting everything
But among the abundance of so much sorrow
Will you be able to face tomorrow?

With hunger, poverty and war
Lord knows who is keeping score
Just be thankful for the Father's son
Who made our lives a Holy one.

To sin, to error and be forgiven
While on this earth are we really living?
Respect, are we giving to one another
To Mom, Dad, Sister and Brother

Through the Eyes of My Joy

What have we contributed to mankind?
Deep down in our hearts what will one find?

As days, weeks, months, and years pass on
And your days on earth have made the run

While looking at the stars, moon, sky and the sun

What will they say?

WELL DONE?

To All my family and friends
Gla – May 2006

LITTLE FELLAS

My heart, it yearns
My stomach churns
When I think about the Little Fellas
My face, it smiles
With every mile
When I think of the Little Fellas
When I first met
The Little Fellas
My eyes, they got to watch them grow
Through sun, rain, sleet, hell and snow
Through Summer, Winter, Fall, and Spring
The Little Fella's into everything
Climb the counter, jump the fence
Growing each day, inch by inch
Still talking about The Little Fellas
As I watch the days, months and years go by
The Little Fellas make me Cry
Not from sadness but from joy
These Little Fellas
Are our Big Boys
All grown up and handsome too!
Ready for the world, What can they do?
Just about anything they desire.
Because we know they've got the power
Black, White, Rich or Poor

Through the Eyes of My Joy

Life will open many doors
But no matter how high they Soar
Our Little Fellas
Go off to War
So as we wake to each new day
For the Little Fellas
WE WILL PRAY!!!!

Gladine Pannel Bruer – August 08, 2006

Through the Eyes of My Joy

Ms. Hicks
To Mother Hicks (One of my Mothers in Christ)
Cherishing her memory always

Remembering Ms. Hicks
She was one of my Picks
A woman of Truth
A woman of Strength
But you didn't dare take her The Length!!!
Because with her firmness and Kind ways
Respect was due her
Each and every day
She stood for what's Right
And frowned on what's Wrong
A woman with a heart
True and Strong
Always making one feel that
They were a part
Rememberiing her is so good for the heart
Remembering Ms. Hicks
A mentor and friend
Remembering her smile
From beginning to end
This poem I dedicate
To Ms. Hicks
A woman who will always be
One of my favorite Picks

Gladine Pannell Bruer – June 2007

Through the Eyes of My Joy

ARE YOU UNHAPPY?

Are you unhappy
Is your unhappiness due to space
Or are you blaming it on your race?
Are you unhappy with everyday life
Boredom, negativity, and strife?
Are your surroundings overwhelming
Full of darkness and misunderstanding?
Are you unhappy with the hand you were dealt?
Have you taken the time to see how others felt?
Is your health bad, are you homeless and sad?
Do you question where your next dollar is from?
Are you classified by the word BUM?
Did you get a chance to see the day start?
Can you hear the thump of your working heart?
If your answer is YES to the last two lines
The five before should be a sign
That in this life, you're doing Just Fine!!!
So why are you unhappy???

To all the unhappy people in this world
GOD BLESS.
Gladine Pannell Bruer – January 2007

AMBIVALENCE

Have you deeply loved and fiercely hated?
Or have you felt eagerly enraptured
and senselessly sad with some person?

Did someone give you comfortable warmth yesterday
But left you feeling cold the next day?
Is it possible that somebody could love you dearly
But look at you as if they don't know you truly?

How does someone give you enduring happiness
But also brings you misery that is immense?

Confusions and questions, all are shrouded in dimensions
Of deceit and misdirections

If only intentions are pure and simple,
these would be no misleading and questions!

Ana Lledo (Friend and Family)

Through the Eyes of My Joy

THE RAIN

Living life, we all have the Pain
That's when you must be able to Walk in the Rain
When your heart is in a strain
You must be ready to take on the Rain
When the body can't connect with the Brain
Take a quiet stroll in the Rain!
Situations you want to rearraign
So take a quick run in the Rain
Your Sanity you are trying to attain
It's time to embrace and grab the Rain
When each day seems to be a ball and chain
Get out and dance in the Rain
Make sure your life is not in vain
Get an umbrella and hold off the Rain
Starting each day with a smile that remains
Even when the day is forecast Rain
Keep your plans simple and plain
So that you can stay out of the Rain
Love-Loyal-Honest and true you will gain
These things will strengthen you in the Rain
Now you know the rules to obtain
So you will know your way in the Rain!

Gladine Pannell Bruer

ANTITHESIS

Yesterday I felt as though I could conquer the world
Today I feel darker than a deep ocean trench
What is the difference between White and Black?
Or greatness and loneliness
or mindfulness and indifferences
When all the sunrises and sunsets
You're meant to survive when all the bliss and sorrow
You're destined to prevail—have you ever thought
among these dreary nights when your tears endlessly fall
the Universe conspired to let you grow
So tell me, Why does everything matter
Get up and brush your luscious hair
Stretch your arms, believe and dare!
Conquer, win and ride the world's Fair

Ana Lledo (Friend and Family)

SPECIAL THAT'S YOU

How do you look at yourself?
Are you confident, loyal, proud and sure,
being transparent and always pure?
Special you are to you
second guess or no question at all
you are the one who makes the call
Second thought or not
You are the one calling the shots
Be yourself, special, whatever you do!
Remember, you just should do YOU

SPECIAL
REMEMBER THAT IS YOU!

Gladine Pannell Bruer

SETTING ONE'S MIND

Be the ones stern of the lessons we learn
Setting one's mind on the goals and expectations
For one's self is the most priority and focus
Grab onto the mindset
For now is the time for
Setting One's Mind!

Gladine Pannell Bruer

Through the Eyes of My Joy

WHO IS D

The fourth letter in the ABC's
To some but not to me!

Who is D
Within my eyes, I see D as a Soul
Of Delightfulness-Dependability-Decent and Dutiful
Driven-Devoted-Deserving-Direct – and a Diva
Within my heart D is Dearest-Dynamic-Dashing-
Dazzling-Doer-Determined-Dedicated-Disciplined-
Daring-Darling-Dreamer-Diligent-
and just right Down-to-Earth
To me this is D

Gladine Pannell Bruer

Through the Eyes of My Joy

SUCH MEMORIES

How fond the thoughts of yesterday
Reminiscence that do not stay
Sentimental of great times—heart, flowers and Sunshine
Smiling and laughter we always yearned
From Granny's advice, we could always learn
that memories are yours to keep and store
To love—cherish and adore
But such memories feel free to keep!
Because sometimes you will ponder and weep!
OH SUCH MEMORIES

Gladine Pannell Bruer

POWERS IS PATIENCE

Keep thee a soft tongue with virtue in mind
Speak of all persons in love and kind
Powerful is patience that we all need to embrace
whenever the time and the place
Patience, a virtue so hold that thought
Powerful it is NO MATTER WHAT!

Gladine Pannell Bruer

IMPRESSIONS OR DIRECTIONS

Impression can be deceptions

Do you know your life's direction?

Your relationship with a person whom

You have trusted

Soon you realize they are corrupted

Instead of believing in one's self first

Deceitful ones will dominate

and thirst on one so simple and pure

that they never give you a chance

To endure the trust, faith, kindness, honesty

SIMPLICITY and love you have for them

Instead your impression and direction has been condemn

Impressions or directions which will it be?

To give you happiness within Thee!

Gladine Pannell Bruer

MEDIA MADNESS

Today is the times of media madness

Politics, war and plenty of sadness

Countries at odds with each other

Killings of Children, father and mothers

No peace, No answers to all the confusion

This time on earth is not an illusion

Just check the media madness

For all the craziness and badness

Peace—democracy and living was great

Now we are all in a horrible state

Will we ever see gladness

Through all the media madness???

Gladine Pannell Bruer

Through the Eyes of My Joy

JUST A SMILE

Start your day off with a smile
Frowns are all so juvenile
Ponder your feelings for a little while
Then decide you are going to smnile
Cherish the thoughts of being pleasant
Instead of hostile
You can conquer whatever the trial
Just by showing that great big smile!

Gladine Pannell Bruer

Exhale or Inhale

Inhale all good
Exhale Bad
Inhale Faith
Exhale Fear
Inhale Love
Be Grateful Always together
We shall prevail

Gladine Pannell Bruer

www.ingramcontent.com/pod-product-compliance
Lightning Source LLC
LaVergne TN
LVHW050027080526
838202LV00069B/6951